A Hat Full of Gold

Written by Lisa Thompson

Pictures by Craig Smith and Lew Keilar

Captain Red Beard was asleep
in his hammock.

He was dreaming
of treasure.

3

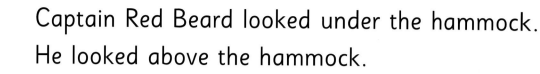

Captain Red Beard looked under the hammock.
He looked above the hammock.

He looked right. He looked left.

There was no sign of his hat.

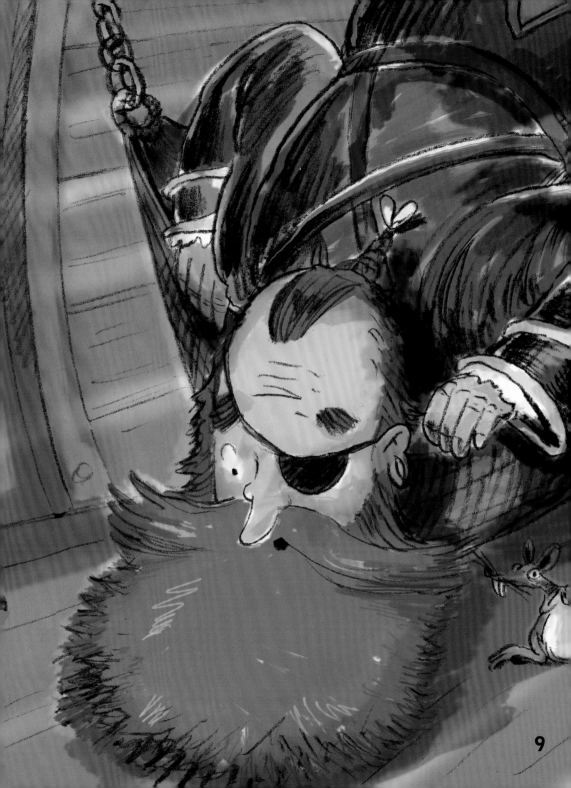

"A hat full of gold for the pirate who finds my hat!" said Captain Red Beard.

"Get to it like flying cannonballs!"

"Dirty rotten pirates," said Fingers the parrot.

She flew around the ship looking for the hat.
She checked between the sails.

She did not find the Captain's hat.

She did find the packet of biscuits she
had been looking for.

Bones checked inside the boxes, the barrels, and the boats.

He did not find the Captain's hat.

He did find the scarf he had been looking for.

Lizzie checked the cabins below deck.

She did not find the Captain's hat.

She did find an old eye patch she had been looking for.

17

"Any sign of my hat?" said the Captain.

"No. We're very sorry Captain," said the crew.

Captain Red Beard looked angry.

He went to get out
of his hammock.

He got tangled
and twisted.

21

THUD! He landed on the floor.

A squashed, black, pirate hat landed on top of him.

Captain Red Beard had been lying on his hat.

"Well it looks like it's a hat full of gold for me!" smiled the Captain.